ISBN: 0-87191-227-9
Library of Congress Catalog Card Number: 72-14173

QUANAH
LEADER OF THE COMANCHE

Julian May

Illustrated by PHERO THOMAS

CREATIVE EDUCATIONAL SOCIETY, Inc.
Mankato, Minnesota 56001

A war party of Comanche and Kiowa braves rode toward a log fort. The Indians knew that this fort held no white soldiers. Instead, there were seven cabins belonging to the Parker family, pioneers who had come to the Comanche lands of east-central Texas the previous year, in 1835.

The war-chief raised a white flag on the end of his lance. In a few minutes, the gate of the fort opened and a white man came out.

"We seek a camping place," said the Indian. "We need water and we are hungry." As he spoke, his men rode nearer and nearer to the fort.

Suddenly, the white man realized what the Indians were doing. He tried to call out a warning to the other settlers, but a flight of arrows brought him down. The red men screamed out their battlecries and galloped into the open gateway.

Mrs. Lucy Parker saw her husband killed. Taking her four children, she tried to flee through the back door of the stockade. After she had gone only a short way, a group of mounted warriors surrounded her. The mother stood helpless as the Indians snatched up her six-year-old son and her nine-year-old daughter and rode away with them.

"Johnny!" cried Mrs. Parker. "Cynthia Ann!"

A neighbor rode up with his rifle and rescued Mrs. Parker and her other two children. But she never saw John and Cynthia Ann again. They were captives of the Comanche, most feared tribe of the southern plains.

Nine years passed. May flowers bloomed among the rich grasses of Laguna Sabinas, a salt lake of West Texas. Their scent filled a Comanche village on the lakeshore and mingled with the smell of tobacco from the medicine man's sacred pipe.

The most important men of the village were gathered in the tipi of a war-leader, the chief's son Peta Nocona. On a rabbit-fur robe in front of the priest lay a baby.

The old man blew puffs of smoke toward heaven, toward earth, and toward the four winds. "Great Spirit, Father, look upon this man-child! Bless the son of Peta Nocona!"

Four times the infant was lifted toward heaven with the prayer: "May he grow up strong!" Then the medicine man gave the child his name. He said: "This is *Quanah, the Sweet-Smelling One.*" The baby was handed to his proud father as the warriors all greeted the child by his new name.

"Quanah! Quanah!"

The mother, Naudah, felt her heart swell with joy. She thought, "My little Quanah will grow up to be a leader of the Comanche, just like his father."

Peta Nocona was a war-leader of the Comanche band known as the Wanderers. They lived for much of the time in the Panhandle country of Texas. But they also roamed from Kansas and Colorado southward as far as Mexico. Their enemies were the man-eating Tonkawas to the south, the Utes to the northwest, and the Apaches to the southwest. The tribe was friendly with the Kiowas to the east and the Cheyenne to the north.

War was a way of life to the Comanche, who grew no crops. They were great horsemen who inhabited the best of the buffalo range. If any other people wanted Comanche land, the Comanche gladly made war on them. It was like a sport to them, a way by which their men gained honor.

In Quanah's birth-year, 1845, the Comanche were at war with white men as well as red. The Indian raids that had begun with the Parker Massacre nine years before had become more and more fierce as pioneers tried to farm the Indian lands.

President Sam Houston of the Republic of Texas tried to make peace with the Indians. Other Texans felt that the only solution to the "Indian problem" lay in wiping out every last red man in the republic.

In 1846, Texas became the twenty-eighth state in the Union. This meant little to the Comanche. A few treaties were signed and the Indians were given presents if they promised to be peaceful. But white settlers continued to homestead Indian land. Even worse, the whites were killing off the buffalo, the most important food of the Comanche.

The Indians became even more angry in 1849, when California gold-seekers cut a new trail right through the heart of the Comanche country. War-leaders such as Peta Nocona led their bands against white settlements more often —killing, scalping, and stealing both horses and human captives.

Some of the older captives were tortured to death. But others, mostly children, were treated more kindly. Some were adopted as full members of the tribe. Others became servants to Comanche chiefs. Peta Nocona and Naudah had a Mexican boy to serve them. He was named Jose, and he helped to care for little Quanah and Quanah's younger brother, Pecos.

Quanah grew to be a handsome boy, somewhat taller than most of the other children. By the time he was eight, he was an expert in the Comanche art of trick riding. He could pick things up from the ground while riding at a full gallop. This was done by hanging from the pony's mane, with only one foot hooked over the horse's back.

The war-leader's son learned to lasso wild mustangs and break them for riding. Adult men more often stole horses in Mexico or in the Apache lands to the west. The Comanche tribe was probably richer in horses than any other North American Indians—and they were the best riders, too.

Quanah also learned to hunt. At first he shot only birds and small animals with a little bow and arrows. As he grew older, he stalked larger game and learned to use a lance as well as a man's bow. Sometimes he and Jose and some of the other boys went off on hunting trips after deer or pronghorns, the fleet little antelopes of the plains.

They frequently saw huge herds of buffalo. But hunting these great animals was not a game for children. In a few years, when Quanah was fifteen or sixteen, he would be allowed to join the tribal buffalo hunt. Each summer and winter, the Comanche bands harvested large numbers of buffalo, taking enough meat and hides to last them for months. The whole band worked hard at this time, the men and older boys doing the hunting, the women and older girls doing the meat-cutting and drying. After the hunts there was always a great feast, with the men bragging about the brave deeds they had done.

When winter came to the southern plains, the Comanche might go south to a warmer climate. If snow caught them, they simply stayed in their large, buffalo-skin tipis. A small fire was all that was needed to keep them snug and warm.

When the cold winds howled around the tipi, Quanah and Pecos liked to listen to their mother tell them stories. The Comanche had many tales about animals who had odd or amusing adventures. And if the boys were naughty, Naudah might tell them to beware of the Great Cannibal Owl, who came at night to eat bad children!

The Indian parents never punished their children. When a boy or girl misbehaved, other members of the tribe made fun of them and shamed them into being good. Quanah seldom got into mischief. It made his mother sad, and he loved Naudah so much that he could not bear to make her unhappy.

By 1858, when Quanah was thirteen, Texas was rapidly filling with settlers from the East. Some of the Texas Indian tribes—including some southern Comanche—were forced onto reservations.

But most of the northern Comanche bands were too proud to give up their old way of life. The white man wanted to turn hunters and warriors into spiritless dirt-scratchers. Never!

Fierce Comanche raiders plundered white settlements and wagon trains. Texas Rangers, together with Tonkawa Indians from the South, were sent to wipe out the Comanche villages and make them submit to reservation life.

One day in May, a mixed force of Rangers and Tonkawas fought with a large group of Comanche north of the Canadian River. The Comanche men were all killed and the women and children taken prisoner.

Then the army turned southward, toward a very large Comanche camp in the Antelope Hills, in what is now western Oklahoma. There the Wanderer band, the Buffalo-Eaters, and the Downstream Band of the Comanche tribe were gathered together. The head chief of this group was old Pohebits Quasho, a famous fighter. Second to him in rank was Peta Nocona, Quanah's father, who was now chief of the Wanderer band.

Quasho's people were the first to meet the enemy. The old chief had a magic shirt that could turn away arrows and ball-shot. He led his warriors out, charging recklessly among the armed Rangers and Tonkawas.

Then a howl of dismay rose from the Comanche braves. Pohebits Quasho had fallen! Warriors tried to lift him from the ground, but enemy bullets drove them away.

Quasho's men were armed only with bows and arrows; they had no chance against the modern guns of the whites. Taking their women and children, they began to flee towards the camp of Peta Nocona.

The Texans came after them—but not before they took a souvenir of the battle. One of the men stripped from Pohebits Quasho's body the magic shirt—an ancient Spanish coat of chain-mail. It had protected the chief from arrows and lead musket balls, but it had not been able to save him from a modern rifle bullet.

When news of the battle reached Peta Nocona, he called his men together quickly.

"We must stop the enemy or slow them down," he said. "Our women and children must have a chance to escape." He told the others of his plan. They would meet the Texan army and lead it to a narrow canyon. Poisoned arrows would be the equal of rifle bullets in such a place.

Nocona's warriors paid heavily as they covered the retreat of their families. Seventy-five men lost their lives before the Texans called it a day and allowed the remaining Comanche to slip away under cover of darkness.

Miles away, in a makeshift camp, Naudah and her sons waited and hoped. The tired defenders straggled in slowly. There were no scalps, no victory songs—only wounds and the heartache of defeat.

Peta Nocona himself was not hurt. He began to make plans at once to move the people to a safer place, for now that Quasho was dead, he had become head chief of the northern Comanche bands.

The next summer, Quanah began to learn the ways of a man. He went on his first community buffalo hunt. His father, the hunt leader, was too busy to watch out for him. So it was the Mexican servant Jose, now a grown man and looking as much like a Comanche as any of them, who showed the chief's son what to do.

First, scouts located the buffalo herd. Then Peta Nocona sent the men and boys to ride quietly around the beasts in a great half-moon. Before the buffalo could smell them, Nocona called out the attack. Screaming hunters began to gallop around and around the herd in an ever-shrinking circle. The buffalo were forced closer and closer together into a compact mass, where they were easy to shoot.

Quanah, waiting on the outer edge of the hunt, was one of the boys supposed to watch for buffalo that might break free. Heart pounding, he sat on his quivering pony while thick dust rose up in the air and the sound of howling men and bellowing buffalo filled his ears.

"Here comes one!" Jose shouted. A big, black bull came charging toward them. Jose lifted his lance, but just then his pony stepped into a prairie-dog hole. The Mexican brave went flying.

Quanah drew an arrow. His well-trained mount followed the bull closely, guided only by the boy's knees. When Quanah was scarcely an arm's breadth away from the buffalo, he let his arrow fly.

The horse swerved quickly out of the way to avoid the sharp horns. When Quanah turned his horse around, he saw the great bull lying dead on the ground, killed by an arrow through the heart.

Jose, who was unhurt, came and stood beside his young master. "Well done, Quanah!" he said. "You are indeed a chief's son."

Peta Nocona and his band kept on raiding white settlements, striking with lightning swiftness and then disappearing before anyone could send for help. Sometimes the Comanche would sweep southward along the Brazos River, into Parker County where relatives of the massacred family lived.

In 1860, Governor Sam Houston sent a small expedition under young Captain Sul Ross to put down the Comanche raiders in the area. Ross trailed Nocona's band to the Pease River and caught up with the Comanche in December.

There the white detachment crept up on the Indian village, where a great buffalo hunt had just ended. The men and women were happy and full of food, and the scouts were not alert. Captain Ross and his men took them by surprise, riding straight into the circle of tipis.

Naudah caught up her infant daughter, Tautahyah. "To the horses!" she shouted to her sons. Peta Nocona was else-were, so she called Jose to help her mount. The Mexican took up a girl servant behind him and they started to gallop after Naudah.

The air was full of rifle fire. One bullet killed the girl riding behind Jose and mortally wounded the Mexican Comanche himself. Cornered by a white soldier, he leaned against a tree and began to sing the Comanche death-song.

Captain Ross demanded that the wounded man surrender. When Jose tried to strike the captain with his lance, another soldier shot the Mexican dead.

"Find out who he was," Ross said to his interpreter. "He was surely a brave one!"

An interpreter turned to a group of captured Comanche women and questioned them. One said: "That was Peta Nocona's Jose."

The interpreter misunderstood. "She says it was the chief, Peta Nocona! Captain, you got old Nocona himself!"

Naudah, with her baby held in one arm, fled from a Ranger officer. When it seemed certain she would be shot, she pulled up her pony and held out the baby. She knew that white men did not often kill children.

The officer brought his prisoner back to the other group of women, where Captain Ross was standing. He came close to Naudah and stared at her face. "This isn't an Indian!" he cried out. "She's a white woman! Look at those blue eyes!"

Naudah did not understand a word. She stood tall and proud, holding her baby, as the two officers discussed her in excited tones. More and more prisoners were brought in, but Naudah was glad that her sons were not among them. Nor was Nocona.

Several days later, Naudah was taken to a fort and cared for by the wives of the soldiers. After asking her many questions through an interpreter, Captain Ross sent for an old man named Isaac Parker. Parker talked to the Indian woman too, then turned to the soldier with tears in his eyes.

"It could be. It could be her, after twenty-four years. Poor little Cynthia Ann!"

The words were familiar to the Indian woman. A small smile lit up her sad face. She placed her hand on her breast.

"Cynthia," she said carefully. "Me—Cynthia."

Miles away, a strong north wind howled around the
tipi of Bends-the-Back, closest friend of Chief Nocona. Several men sat around a small fire. One of them was Nocona
himself, badly wounded.

"You must choose another," Nocona said, "for I know that I will not live to see the spring grass. Now the people are scattered and the white soldiers are everywhere. I am glad that I can no longer be chief. Because I think that now the Wanderers will be able to wander no more. We will have to go to the reservation just as the others have done."

Some of the men cried, "No!" But Bends-the-Back said, "They have guns and we have none. How can we hope to drive them from our land?"

Off in the shadows, a boy who was supposed to be asleep listened to the men talk. Quanah's eyes filled with tears as his father spoke of death. He had lost his beloved mother, his little sister, his good friend Jose. Now would his father be taken from him as well? Orphans did not fare well among the Comanche. Most of them lived lives of lonely poverty.

And was it true—that the Wanderers would be confined to one place and made to become farmers? An anger even bigger than his sorrow started to grow in Quanah's heart.

One of the older men said, "At least in the reservation there is food. What will become of us this winter, now that we have lost all our buffalo meat? It is better to submit than starve."

Quanah jumped up, forgetting that boys must never interrupt men. He cried out: "I would gladly starve!" He stood tall and bronze in the firelight, flames lighting up his gray eyes and shining on his reddish-brown hair.

"You may change your mind about that some day," his father said.

The next spring, as he had foretold, Chief Peta Nocona died. Indian custom now asked a terrible price of his young sons. To prove their grief, they had to give away all of their possessions. And to insure that the spirit of their dead father would not return to haunt the people, they had to leave the Wanderers and go to live with other Comanche bands.

Little Pecos was given to the Buffalo-Eater band. But he had never been a strong child, and he soon took sick and died. Quanah went to the fierce Antelope band, dwellers on the windswept Staked Plains. There he lived for several years as a lonely herd-boy, caring for the band's horses until the day that he became a warrior.

With the taking of his first enemy scalp, his taboo would be lifted and he would be a man.

Many miles away, Naudah and her baby daughter were being cared for by the Parker family. As the long months passed, the sad-faced woman slowly learned English. Dim memories of the long-ago massacre came back to her and she knew that she was really the lost Cynthia Ann. But this did not mean that she could accept the white man's way of life. At heart, she was a Comanche. She never smiled and often begged the Parkers to return her to the Indian people so that she could search for her two sons.

"We'll take you back, Cynthia Ann," Isaac Parker promised. "Just as soon as the war is over." Cynthia Ann did not understand that Texas was caught up in the Civil War. For three years she pleaded; but both she and her little daughter died in 1864, a year before the end of the war between the states. A fever took the life of little Tautahyah —but Cynthia Ann Parker died of a broken heart.

Texas elected to join the Confederacy during the Civil War. The Confederate government signed a treaty of peace with the northern Comanche bands—except the diehard Antelopes. The Indians said they would stay on a reservation and stop raiding. The whites promised to give the red men cattle and supplies and help them learn a new way of life.

But as the war went on, Texas sent its troops to fight Union soldiers. The Indians discovered that there was no one to stop them from going back to their raiding—and so they started to destroy the settlements again.

The Civil War in Texas did not feature much fighting beween Union and Confederate troops. But there was a great deal of bloodshed on the northwestern frontier, where the Indian raids devastated the ranches and farms.

Quanah, with the Antelope people, roamed through a territory with very few white settlements. The Indians and the buffalo knew the secret waterholes of the Staked Plains, but the whites did not. So the Indians ruled this territory and used it as a base for raiding. They fought against the Apaches and also stole Texas cattle and sold them to Comancheros, Spanish-speaking traders of New Mexico.

It was on a raid against the Apache that Quanah became a man. He killed an enemy brave with his lance, scalped the man, and took his horse.

Later, in the Comanche camp, the great warriors of the band sat in a half-circle. A buffalo hide was on the ground. Victory-dancers chanted and pranced to the beat of drums.

Young Quanah, riding his horse, came into the warrior's circle. He thrust his spear into the buffalo hide and at once the music and dancing stopped. Everyone waited while Quanah told of his brave deed. Other witnesses agreed that the young man told the truth.

"Come down and join the company of warriors," the war chief proclaimed. "Now you are no longer a boy, but a man!"

The dancing and the singing resumed. And Quanah, still in his teens, was accepted as an Antelope warrior.

Because he was an orphan, without powerful and rich relatives to help him, Quanah was driven to strive harder for honor and glory than the other youths did. In 1867, when he was 22, he rose to the rank of sub-chief, at the head of a group of young men his own age.

He took sick with fever and could not go with the warriors on their summer raid. So when he recovered in autumn, he decided to go to the great council of southern plains tribes that had been called by the Great Father of Washington. The Comanche, the Kiowa, the Cheyenne, the Arapaho, and the Kiowa-Apache tribes sent representatives to Medicine Lodge, in Kansas. No Antelope chiefs attended, but they wanted Quanah to find out what was happening.

The council met for several weeks, the chiefs and the white Indian Commissioners taking turns making speeches. The Indians told tales of broken white promises, invasion of Indian land, and the killing of the buffalo. The whites wanted the Indians to stop murdering settlers and stealing and burning their property.

A white general told the chiefs: "The time has come for you to live in peace or face destruction by white armies." Other officials told the Indians they would receive reservation land, schools, farm equipment, cattle, and supplies for a period of 30 years.

After much talking, the chiefs agreed to sign the Treaty of Medicine Lodge. The Comanches would go to a three-million-acre reservation in the southern part of the Indian Territory (now Oklahoma). Ten Comanche chiefs put their marks on the white man's paper. Quanah spoke to them with contempt.

"You old men have already won your warrior honors. You have many horses and now you will have the white man's gifts. But what about young men like me? How can we win honor if we are farmers?"

Quina Bivi, chief of the Wanderers, said: "The old days are gone, Quanah. We will have to seek a new kind of honor."

"Not I," Quanah replied. "I'll go back to the Antelopes and live in the old way."

Now Quanah embarked on a career as a famous raider of white settlements. And he was not alone. Most of the northern Comanche and Kiowas did not stay on the reservation. The food and supplies were often late or poor in quality. As the Indian raids went on, reservation supplies were cut down still more to "pay for" the raids.

The buffalo were fast disappearing. More and more settlers poured into Texas from the war-ravaged eastern states. White settlers demanded that the Indian raids be stopped, and the army was sent to crush the Comanche.

In 1874, when the people were hungry and desperate, a holy man named Ishatai came to the Antelope band, where Quanah was now a great war chief. Ishatai told the Comanche that they should hold a Sun Dance, as the Kiowas and Cheyenne did. This would give them great power and enable them to sweep the whites away.

A mighty medicine was made at the Sun Dance. Then nearly a thousand warriors of the Comanche, Cheyenne, and Kiowa tribes rode off to the trading post of Adobe Walls to start the great war against the white men.

It was dawn when Quanah led his charging warriors toward the trading post. Arrows took the lives of two white traders and their large dog, which tried to protect them. The Indians scalped all three. The other white men were safe inside the fort, sniping at the Indians with powerful buffalo guns.

On a hill some distance away, Ishatai watched through the day as the Indians tried vainly to take the trading post. He and his pony were smeared with "bulletproof" paint, but the prophet loftily declined to enter the battle. The chiefs began to mutter. Where was the easy victory they had been promised?

On the next day, a freak shot traveled a long distance and killed Ishatai's horse. Quanah looked at the medicine man with scorn.

"Where is your powerful medicine now?" he asked.

Ishatai tried to excuse himself. But the Comanche chief turned from him coldly and led his men back to the fastness of the Staked Plains.

A hot, dry summer followed. The people suffered hunger and thirst, and Quanah remembered the words he had spoken so long ago to his dying father. But freedom was still dearer to the Comanche than life itself. So they fled the soldiers when they could and fought when they had to.

Time and again the white troops fell upon the Comanche villages, destroying tipis and food, shooting the Indians' horses. And still the Antelope people refused to go to the reservation.

The Indian agent sent messages: "Come in to the reservation and you will no longer suffer. But if you keep on fighting, you will surely die."

When winter approached, many of the Comanche bands decided to surrender rather than see their families starve or freeze. Still Quanah would not give up.

He led his people southward to escape one of the worst winters in Texas history. But the women and children had a very hard time. In spring they returned to the Staked Plains and there Quanah met with representatives of the Indian Commission who tried once more to convince the chief to come to the reservation.

Quanah turned away from the white men, sorrow and anger welling up in his heart. These were his mother's people. Their blood ran in his veins. Now they told him that he was the last chief to refuse the new life. His was the last wild Comanche band.

At last he made up his mind. And later that spring, on June 2, 1875, Quanah rode into Fort Sill and surrendered.

"We will take up the white man's way," he said.

Unlike some tribes of the East, the Comanche had adopted very few of the white man's customs and inventions. They were people with a stone-age culture suddenly called upon to walk a strange and often frightening road toward civilization.

At first, Quanah was saddened and bitter because he had been forced to surrender. But he was a chief and his people needed a leader who could help them learn the white man's way. Quanah decided that the first thing he would do was visit his mother's family.

The Indian agent at Fort Sill gave him a note to carry on his journey into Texas. It said: *This young man is the son of Cynthia Ann Parker. He is going to visit his mother's people. Please show him the road and help him as you can.*

All of Texas seemed to know the story of Cynthia Ann. Quanah rode for many days and finally reached the home of Silas Parker, Cynthia Ann's younger brother. The family welcomed the tall Indian and asked him to stay with them. He lived with the Parkers all summer and learned to speak English. At night, he slept in Cynthia Ann's bed and dreamed of her.

And in her honor, he took a new name. From now on, he would call himself Quanah Parker.

When he returned to the Indian Territory, Quanah knew a great deal more about white civilization than before. He was ready to help his people and give them advice when they brought him their troubles.

Old Moway, the head chief, came to Quanah in 1878. "I am old," he said. "Now it is time for another to lead the people. All of the chiefs together have chosen you, even though you are still a young man. Your white blood will be a bridge for us."

And so it was. Quanah urged the families to send their children to school, where the boys learned ranching and the girls modern housekeeping. He found a way to combat the rustlers who were stealing the tribe's horses. When the buffalo finally disappeared, he worked out an agreement with Texas cattlemen: the Indians would let the white men's stock graze on the reservation. In return, the Indians would be paid in cattle. Within a few years, the tribe had a large herd of cattle and Quanah Parker was a friend to some of the most important ranchers in northern Texas.

As a head chief, Quanah was entitled to four wives by tribal law. Each had a separate tipi, set up around the chief's own. Handsome sons and daughters were born. When the time came, Quanah sent them to school—first on the reservation, and later to the famous Indian School in Carlisle, Pennsylvania. He was becoming very prosperous; two of his daughters married wealthy cattlemen.

His people were not doing so well, however. Many still clung to the old ways and longed for the days of the buffalo hunts and the wandering. They were not happy as farmers and many of them, unlike Quanah, could not easily follow the white man's road.

An Indian court of justice was set up in 1886 and Quanah was appointed one of the judges. He adopted more and more of the white man's ways. From the tipi, he moved to a large house with stars painted on the roof.

Meanwhile, land-hungry white settlers demanded that the reservation be opened to homesteaders. Quanah's friends, the cattle-barons, helped fight this movement because they didn't want "nesters" carving up the range into little farms. However, in 1892, some chiefs finally signed the Jerome Agreement, which would give each Indian 160 acres of land, while the rest would be opened to settlement. Quanah did not sign this agreement, and when he learned of it, he was furious.

He gathered together the chiefs who had signed and told them that they had done a bad thing. "Our people are not yet ready to live like white men. Our children still have much to learn about farming and raising cattle."

Quanah wanted the government to allow the Indians to lease their land to the whites for grazing, but not give it up completely. He himself went to Washington to explain to the President why he thought this was the best plan. Grover Cleveland promised to help him, and for awhile, the Jerome Agreement was set aside.

In 1897, the 30 years of the Medicine Lodge Treaty came to an end. Once again, Quanah went to the Capitol to ask that the reservation system be continued.

"My people are not yet ready to live as independent citizens," he said. "Maybe half are ready, but not all."

He was fighting a losing battle. Other parts of the Indian Territory had filled with homesteaders. There was a strong movement to make the territory into a new state, named Oklahoma. And on June 6, 1900, Congress made the Jerome Agreement the law of the land.

Quanah rushed to Washington, but President McKinley told him: "You yourself have said that the Indians must learn to live with the white men. Now the time has come."

And he walked away.

With the coming of the white homesteaders, towns sprang up almost overnight on the reservation. White churches were built and missionaries sent to the Indians. Quanah saw that the "Jesus road" was good. Although he did not become a Christian, many of his children did. And the chief told his people that this religion would help them.

The Comanche chief continued to fight for the rights of his tribe. He became a close friend of the new President, Teddy Roosevelt. Many honors were given to him, and he became a wealthy man. But now old age was upon him and most of his children were grown up. Some had married Indians, some had married whites.

In 1907 he went back to Laguna Sabinas to fulfill the Comanche custom of sleeping three nights in his birth-place before he died. The last time he had seen the place, he had been a naked young man riding a pony. Now he was 63, dressed in the white man's clothes, and riding in a handsome automobile.

He was finally able to fulfill his mother's dearest wish, more than 40 years after her death. In 1910, the remains of Cynthia Ann Parker and her infant daughter were transferred from Texas to an Indian cemetery in Oklahoma. Naudah lay among her people at last.

Quanah Parker himself died on February 23, 1911, after a short illness. He was the last chief of the Comanche. As a great Indian leader, he had done his best to build for his people a bridge between the red man's world and the white.